D1569382

Discovering
SELF-CONFIDENCE

Getting to know yourself can increase your self-confidence.

Discovering SELF-CONFIDENCE

Patricia Kramer

THE ROSEN PUBLISHING GROUP, INC.

NEW YORK

Published in 1991 by The Rosen Publishing Group, Inc.
29 East 21st Street, New York, NY 10010

First Edition
Copyright 1991 by Patricia Kramer

Printed in Hong Kong
Manufactured in Hong Kong

Library of Congress Cataloging-in-Publication Data

Kramer, Patricia M.,
    Discovering self-confidence / by Patricia Kramer.
    (The Self-esteem library)
    Includes bibliographical references and index.
    Summary: Explains how self-esteem and self-confidence can be achieved and maintained.
    ISBN 0-8239-1275-2
    1. Self-confidence. 2. Self-respect. 3. Teenagers—Conduct of life. [1. Self-confidence. 2. Self-respect. 3. Conduct of life.]
I. Title. II. Series.
BF575.S39K63   1990
158′.1—dc20

90-49447
CIP
AC

Contents

Introduction

"I am just who I was meant to be;

I will look forward to the challenges of today

with hope and strength,

And know that I am able to meet them."

—Anonymous

Do you remember Popeye the sailorman? He was always saying, *"I yam what I yam what I yam."* What he was really saying is, "This is who I am. I accept myself as I am." He was telling us, "What you see is what you get." He wanted to be accepted just as he was.

This book is about believing in yourself. Believing in yourself and accepting yourself as you are is called self-confidence. It's having faith in what you say and do. It's being sure of yourself and trusting yourself. It's also being comfortable with your emotions and your feelings.

Confidence is feeling good about the decisions you make. Usually, we gain self-confidence as we grow up. But not all adults have self-confidence. Things happen in our lives that affect our confidence. Sometimes things happen that keep us from believing in our abilities. It may occur when we are tiny babies, young children, or even teenagers. Whatever it is, it keeps us from ever feeling good about ourselves.

How, when, or where does self-confidence begin? What does it take for a young person to grow up to be a successful, happy, and healthy adult? What gets in the way?

This book will look at all the things that can affect your self-confidence. We will explore many of the events that happened to you as you were growing up. We will find out whether the things that happened during your childhood helped or hurt your self-confidence. We will also look at all the things that help us to build and keep self-confidence. Believing that you are capable, that you can achieve, and that you are a good person is the key to success. If you do not believe in yourself, you probably will have little chance of succeeding in life. If you do not believe in yourself, no one else will either.

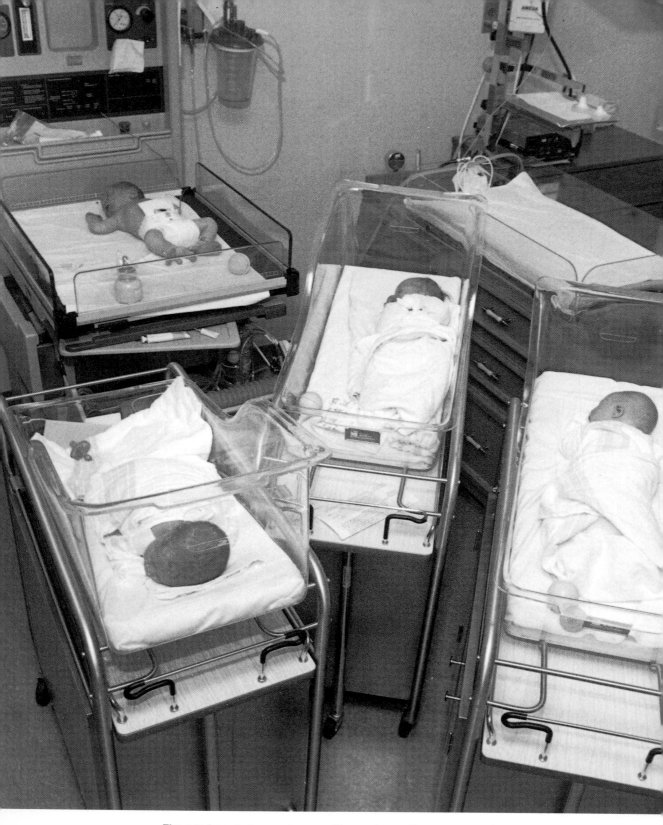

The newborn baby receives positive and negative messages in its very first hours of life.

Chapter 1
Childhood Messages

"Perhaps the most important single cause of a person's success or failure has to do with the question of what he believes about himself".

-Arthur W. Combs

Wouldn't it be terrific if we were all born feeling great about ourselves? Well, we are! It's what happens from then on that causes us to feel differently. Researchers don't know how early in our lives we begin to understand. They don't know how early we are affected by what people say. It may start when you're newly born and still in the hospital. The people around you send many messages. Some of those messages are loving and kind, but some are unkind and even cruel. Some come from your parents. What if your dad said, "I wanted a son. What am I going to do with a daughter?" What if you overheard one of your relatives saying, "What a pity, she's such a homely baby. I hope she outgrows it." Many people believe that babies don't understand. But what if they're wrong?

If childhood messages do influence us, then we might want to better understand why people say and do the things they do. Why does someone say negative or unpleasant things?

Generally, people don't treat others badly unless something bad happened to them at one time. Usually people act mean because they don't feel very good about themselves. They heard so many negative messages that they began to believe they were true.

If your parents were treated badly when they were young, they may not have learned to be kind. They may not know how to say or do nice things to you or your brother(s) or sister(s). Because their parents or people around them treated them badly with words or with things they did, they now repeat that same behavior. This is very sad.

The best thing that could happen would be to repeat only the good things. It's a shame to pass on bad things. When you hear only unkind words, you believe them. Then you feel inclined to say them yourself. When you do, you continue the cycle.

For example: How would you feel if your mom often said to you: "You sure are lazy," or "Why can't you get good grades like your brother, Mark? He's so smart"? Sooner or later, you might begin to believe the things that she said about you. You might become lazy or not work very hard in school or not care about your grades. Sometimes you make it happen because you believe it. It is called a "self-fulfilling prophecy."

Other Reasons People Are Unkind

People also may say unkind things because of their bad mood. For example, if your parents have a good day at work, or if something nice happened to them, they may be in a good mood. Then they probably say nice things. But if something bad happened to them, they may be very upset and get into a bad mood.

Child abuse often is the only resort of parents who were themselves abused in childhood.

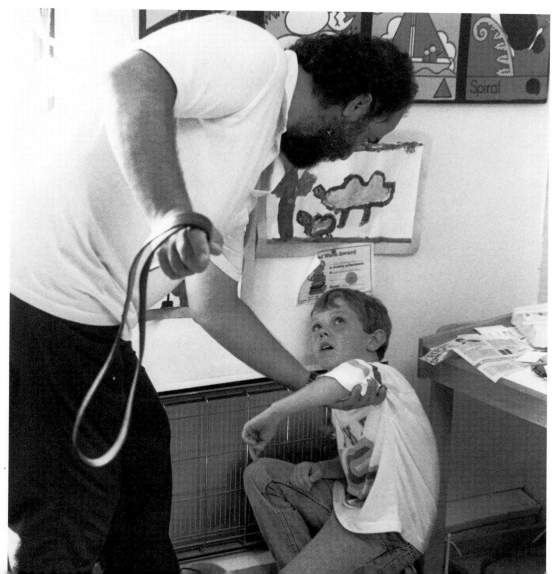

When people are in a bad mood they sometimes say unkind things. Usually they don't mean those things.

If your parents were upset or angry with you because you wouldn't stop crying or wouldn't eat, they may have said things that weren't very nice. If they got a note from a teacher that you weren't behaving, they probably were upset. They may have said something unkind like "What's the matter with you? Can't you ever behave?" Even if they were angry at someone else, they may have taken it out on you.

Self-Esteem

Can you be a very capable person and still have little confidence? Some people do many things very well. Still, they have no confidence in themselves, because their self-esteem is low. Do you think it possible to believe in yourself in some areas and not feel confident in others? The answer is yes. Can a brain surgeon be a good mechanic? Of course, but if the brain surgeon couldn't fix cars, would he/she then have no self-confidence? Or would he/she understand that no one can be good at everything?

Some people have many talents and can do all kinds of things. Others develop excellent skills in one or two areas and not in others. Some can do many things, but none of them very well. Have you ever heard the expression, *"Jack of all trades, master of none"?* These people may be very self-confident because of their various skills even though they don't excel at anything. They believe in themselves.

Chapter 2
Self-Control

Sometimes neglected children find that they get attention

by acting out—by losing control.

When you were a baby, you had no control over your emotions or your needs. You couldn't control your muscles, so your arms and legs waved in the air. You probably looked a little like a bug on its back. You couldn't even control your bathroom habits, and that's why you wore diapers. When you were upset, uncomfortable, hungry, or wet, you cried until you got the attention of someone who could help you.

Do you have control over your emotions now? Do you say or do anything you want whenever you want? Can you control your feelings when you get frustrated? What about when you get mad? Do you throw temper tantrums? Do you sometimes get so angry that you boil over? Some people never learn self-control. They have never matured.

There are many reasons that some young people never grow up. Maybe as young children they never got much attention. Everyone was just too busy. Perhaps both parents worked and weren't at home much. Or their parents were divorced. Sometimes neglected children find that they get attention by acting out—by losing control. So they learn to act in ways that get attention—even if it is negative.

Other children are overprotected. They may not be allowed to do anything for themselves. They may not be allowed to make any decisions for themselves. Someone is nearly always with them. Someone is usually telling them what to do. These children don't learn responsibility. Most overprotective parents love their children. They believe that they are doing what's best for them. They're afraid that something will happen to their children if they let them do anything or go anywhere. Overprotective parents can often do as much harm as parents who are not available to their children. The result can be children who never learn self-control. They simply do not grow up. Could you be one of those children?

Finish these sentences and see what you learn about your self-control.

I get mad when . . .
When I am angry I . . .
Three things that make me angry are . . .

Then answer yes or no to the following questions on a separate piece of paper. Answer quickly without thinking too much about your answer. When you've finished, think about your answers.

I lose my temper easily. Yes ___ No___
I get angry a lot. Yes___ No___
I am easily frustrated. Yes___ No___
My emotions control me. Yes___ No___
I am unable to control my feelings. Yes___ No___
People can push my buttons easily. Yes___ No___
I say whatever I think. Yes___ No ___
My teachers probably think I have no self-control.
Yes___ No___
I get into a lot of fights. Yes___ No___
I fight with my parents a lot. Yes___ No___

What did you learn about yourself? Did you discover anything new? Were you pleased with your answers? Or did you find some things about yourself that you are not very proud of? If you did, it may be time to think of ways to learn self-control. What are some things that might help you be more in control? Make a list of at least five. Then add as many more as you can. Put your list where you can see it everyday. Then start practicing. It won't be easy to develop self-control, but it will be worth it.

Angry youngsters need to learn self-control.

Belief in yourself often comes from knowing yourself.

Chapter 3

Believing in You

"If I am not for myself, who will be?"

-Hillel

What you believe is true often becomes true for you. If what you believe is negative, something negative may happen. There is a saying, *"What you believe, you achieve."* If you believe that you are capable, responsible, and able to achieve, you will be those things. But it works both ways. If you think of yourself as a failure, you may become a failure.

Sometimes the beliefs that we hold are not really true. If you have constantly been told that you will fail, you may start to fail. You then prove they were right. If you have always been told that you are stupid, you'll probably start acting stupid. If you were told that you were lazy, irresponsible, clumsy, unable to do anything right, guess what—you may become all those things. But those beliefs are simply not true.

Even if you sometimes act those ways—everyone does—it is not true all the time. The question is how you can change what you believe. How can you believe more positive things about yourself?

Here's an exercise you can start with. It may help you to recognize what you can already do. Starting with the words, "I can . . .," think of as many endings as possible (at least ten). For example:

I can use a computer.
I can play basketball.
I can sew.
I can make friends easily.

I bet you can make a list a mile long if you really let your imagination go wild.

You can also start a success log. A log simply is a daily record. You've heard about a ship's log in which the captain lists all that happens each day while at sea. Well, put everything that you do that turns out okay in your log. List even simple successes. For example:

Monday, January 10
Today I made my bed.
Today I kept a secret for a friend.
Today I didn't scream at my mother (little brother, sister).
Today I didn't cut any classes.
Today I was on time to three classes.

Tuesday, January 11
Today I was on time to all my classes.

You see, successes don't have to be big ones. You may think that if you don't get straight As or make the team, you haven't succeeded. But that's not true. Anytime you do something well, finish a task, solve a problem, or make a good decision, you have succeeded. You have to start seeing things that way. Then you will start to see yourself as a success. When you see yourself as a success, guess what? You become one. Remember the saying, *"What you believe, you achieve."* Tuck that little thought away somewhere and think about it often.

Perfection

We're always trying to be perfect. But there's no such thing. No one is perfect. We all make mistakes sometimes. Having confidence in yourself doesn't mean that you will never make a mistake. Actually, having self-confidence means exactly the opposite. A person with self-confidence knows that being human means he/she is not perfect. He/she knows that it is all right to make a mistake. And the person with confidence knows that when a mistake is made, it can be corrected. Many people feel a need to be right. They can't admit their own mistakes. Sadly, in order to be right, they must prove others wrong. So keep trying to excel in whatever you attempt, but don't expect perfection from yourself or others.

One of your early roles in life will be as a student.

Chapter 4

Roles

If you can develop your confidence and ability to meet the roles ahead, you will find your adult years exciting.

A person with confidence is always flexible. Being flexible means that you are able to move back and forth between roles, ideas, and beliefs. It means that you may not agree with someone else's ideas, but you will listen to them. And you will respect that person's right to have them. You will respect others' rights to be different from you. You will allow someone else to feel different. And you can still be friends. You know that differences do not mean right or wrong. They're only different.

For example:

A role is the way you act when you are with different people or in different situations. When we think of the word "role," we usually think about actors in movies or on television. They play the parts of different people. Sometimes an actor is the "good guy" in

A very satisfying role for a young girl is that of daughter to a loving mother.

one film and an "evil person" in another. The same actor can play many different roles.

In real life people play many different roles, too. Being a friend is one kind of role. When you're in class as a student, you're in another role. When you go to work, your role is that of employee. At home, you are a son, daughter, sister, or brother. When you are in a romantic relationship, you are in still another role—a boyfriend or girlfriend. When you get married, you will be a husband or wife. If you have children, you will be a parent. And one day you may be a boss, and then your role will be that of employer. Those are some of the roles you may play in your life.

A self-confident person is as comfortable talking to an employer as he/she is to a friend. But the confident person knows the difference, too. He/she knows that there is a time to be friendly and a time to be serious. It would not be right to talk to an employer about personal matters the way you might talk to a friend. Soon you will be an adult. If you can develop your confidence and ability to meet the roles ahead, you will find your adult years exciting. You will also achieve the success that is yours for the asking.

Your job as a babysitter can be an important experience.

Exercise is an essential part of any program of fitness.

Chapter 5

Fitness

(Nutrition, Exercise, and Good Health)

If you want to be considered self-confident, you must look like someone with self-confidence.

People with self-confidence know that one way to feel good about themselves is to look well and feel well. They don't have to be handsome or a bathing beauty. They do know that they have to feel fit. They know they must eat right. They don't skip meals. They don't eat too much junk food. They know that the wrong food can damage their skin and too much food can get their bodies out of shape.

Self-confident people know how important it is to keep their bodies in good shape. They know they must have a good exercise program or just be active. An easy way to be active is to get involved in sports. Or you can take long walks, swim, jog, or work out to an exercise tape. Keeping fit means paying attention to your diet, activity level, and health. Fitness will also affect your skin and your hair. In fact, everything about you will look different when you are in good shape.

Hygiene, too, affects the way you look and feel about yourself. Hygiene means cleanliness. Most of us don't have to be reminded about cleanliness. But every once in a while we may get lazy or sloppy. When we do, our appearance suffers. Maybe your hair is dirty. You might forget to change clothes or shower, which could result in body odor. Maybe you forget to brush your teeth and get bad breath. The final result can be rotten teeth.

If you want to be considered self-confident, then you must *look* like someone with self-confidence. Your clothes must be clean and pressed. They should fit you well—not too big, not too small, not too tight. Looking fashionable doesn't mean looking sloppy or crude.

Proving Yourself (Do I Need Approval?)

A person with self-confidence does not need to prove him/herself to anyone else. You are able to make your own decisions based on what you believe to be right. Most often, those ideas come from what you have been taught by your family. If you are comfortable with who you are, you do not need to act the way others want you to. Trying to feel the way others think you should can only cause you to be let down. When you try to feel a certain way—and don't—you may feel depressed. The more comfortable you are with yourself, the less you will feel the need for approval from others. You will know what is right or wrong in your own heart.

Chapter 6

Shyness

What can a shy person do to overcome his or her shyness? First, shy people need to understand that they have choices.

Think of a turtle when it feels threatened. It pulls its head back into its shell. Well, people act that way sometimes, too. Most of us have been in situations where we have felt uncomfortable. We didn't know what to say. There were people we didn't know. We probably didn't have self-confidence at those times. We probably felt **shy** and withdrew into our shells. Shy to many of us means "out of our comfort zone." That means the space that we feel comfortable in with people who we know will accept us.

There are many ideas about what makes someone shy. Of course, no one is certain. It may come from overprotective parents. They may have kept their children from anything they thought would harm them or might be difficult for them. Maybe the kids were afraid they couldn't do anything on their own so they stayed to themselves.

One might become shy from being bullied. When you're too small, too big, or heavier than others your age, sometimes other kids bully you. If you're ill, out of school, and unable to be with other students, you may withdraw. When you're finally back with other students, you feel shy—sort of out of it. If you were raised without many friends near you, you may have learned to play by yourself. Then when you are around others, you feel shy. Young people with disabilities often feel uncomfortable around their peers. A disability can be blindness, deafness, loss of a limb, or a disease that affects the way you look. Disabilities make people feel self-conscious. They may be afraid they are going to be made fun of. Rather than have that happen, people withdraw—just like a turtle. It's easier to avoid people than have to go through the pain.

Generally, shy people lack self-confidence. What can a shy person do to overcome his or her shyness? First, shy people need to understand that they have choices. Usually it is what we say to ourselves that makes us act or feel as we do. Shyness may result from the words that you say to yourself about a certain event or person. It's called **self-talk.**

For example:

If you are walking down the street alone and say to yourself, "I am scared; if someone tries to mug me, what will I do?" you will probably be very scared. If while walking down the same street you say, "I know that it is safe here and there are police around if I need them," you won't be so scared.

With good friends, a disability need not cause you to withdraw from society.

Or if you say, "I'm so embarrassed. I just know everybody is looking at me; they're probably laughing because I wear a leg brace," you will probably be embarrassed. But if you say to yourself, "I know that I have a disability; when they get to know me, they'll know that I'm just like them," you won't be embarrassed.

Or if you wake up and say to yourself, "I know today is going to be a lousy day; I know that everybody in my class is going to make fun of me," you'll probably have a lousy day. Then you'll withdraw and people might really make fun of you.

If you convince yourself that you can't make friends for any reason, you'll probably go into your shell—like the turtle. You can talk yourself into being shy.

Only you can turn your shyness around. You can develop your self-confidence by positive self-talk. Try it. Write down five things about yourself that you don't like or you think people don't like about you. Then rewrite those things using positive self-talk.

For example:

Negative: *I'm fat, and people don't like fat people.*

Positive: *I know that I am a little overweight, but I'm still fun to be with.*

Negative: *I'll never be very smart because I can't read very well.*

Positive: *I have a reading problem that I'm working on. But people sure like to hear me play the guitar.*

Another way to work on your shyness is to make a list of all the things that you wish you could do. Include places you want to go and people you would like to meet or talk to. Then rewrite your list in a positive way as if those things had already happened. Be specific about what you want to happen.

For example:

I would like to be able to go someplace alone.

I feel great about going to the school cafeteria by myself.

I wish I could talk to that cute boy/girl in my class.

I really enjoy talking to _____ in my math class.

I wish I didn't worry that people will make fun of me.

Even though I have a slight limp, I feel great about the way people accept me.

After you complete your list, make a decision to try each one—one at a time. Write down a realistic date next to each one as a goal for yourself. Don't feel you must do them all or overcome all your feelings right away. But don't put off trying by saying, "I can't," "I'll feel foolish if I try," or "I know someone will laugh at me if I do."

Try doing all the things that you would like to do.

The bully is really afraid of being found out as a coward.

Chapter 7

Inferiority-Superiority Complex

There really is no such thing as a superiority complex.

Are you a bully? Are you someone who picks on others? Maybe it is someone smaller than you or less active in sports. People often become bullies because they lack self-confidence. They may come on as tough, cool, and really with it. Often people think bullies have a "superiority complex."

Really, most bullies are exactly the opposite. They have inferiority complexes. They appear strong and cocky, but they really are very scared inside. They're afraid that they will be found out. Their biggest fear is that others will discover they're not as tough as they appear. They're really not tough at all. They keep up their disguise by putting others down. They fight or say cruel, mean, or untrue things. That may be their way to feel better about themselves.

People with self-confidence don't need to do that. They learn to accept faults. Self-confident people know what they can do. They continue to try to do better and learn what they don't know. There really is no such thing as a superiority complex. Remember that if you think you are better than anyone else, it is usually because you don't think much of yourself. If you are bothered physically or verbally by a "bully," just think of that person as someone who doesn't really like him/herself. He needs to try to make you look bad so that he can look better in others' eyes. What the bully doesn't recognize is that he/she looks like a fool and doesn't win friends, anyway.

Write a Résumé

You know how important self-confidence can be when you are trying to sell yourself. You may be interviewing for a job. You have to convince people that you are deserving, qualified, or interesting. You have to find a way to make people believe that you are the "right" person for the job.

Take some time when your homework is done and find a place where no one will bother you. Think about all of your qualities even if they seem unimportant. Be honest. You might want to make a list of all your good traits first.

Write a *résumé*, a summary of all your *qualifications*, as if you were applying for a real job. Here's an example:

John Smith/Jane Doe
Anywhere USA
Born: July 30, 1974
Health: Excellent

1989 to Present: High school student for past three years. I have
received all As and Bs in English, history, social studies, and,
most important, conduct. I have gotten Cs in science and math
but continually try to improve my grade. I have been active in 4-H
and Student Council. I'm particularly interested in the following
sports: baseball, track, volleyball. I'm first string on the baseball
team as right fielder and second string in volleyball. I have a job
working as a bag boy/girl at the supermarket. I get along well
with most people. I am a good and loyal friend.

1985–1988   Attended Paul Jr. High/Middle School. I received Bs and
Cs in all my classes. I liked English and history the most. My
favorite sports were baseball and volleyball, but I didn't make the
teams. I played the violin in the school band. I was a boy/girl
scout and a member of a hiking club, and I collected stamps.
I did jobs like walking my neighbors' pets, mowing lawns and
cleaning sidewalks when it snowed. I got along well with others.

1979–85   Attended Brightwood Elementary School. I was an average
student, but I did work hard in class. I did my homework most of
the time. I got mostly Bs and Cs. I played volleyball and soccer
at school. I began stamp collecting.

Hobbies: Stamp collecting, skating, sewing, mechanics, model
building.

Goals and Ideals: I would like to go to college and learn to study
business. I would like to own my own business someday. I
would like to get a job with a company where I could learn about
running a business. I am willing to start doing simple tasks.
I realize that I have to learn from the bottom up. I am a hard
worker and I learn fast. I am loyal. I am almost always on time.
I know that I have to prove myself first. Any company that hires
me will be proud to have me as an employee.

35

Values

Do you know what your values are? It is hard to have self-confidence without knowing your own values. Your values are your beliefs, morals, customs, and ideals. They usually come from your family and the surroundings where you were raised. When you are growing up, you usually believe in the values of your family. Sometimes young people question the values of their parents. Some people believe that teens should never question what they have been taught. Others believe that wanting to question the values of our parents shows maturity. They believe that young people who prove their maturity should be able to make their own decisions.

Sometimes as adults, we continue to question our values. We may choose to change them based on our own experiences. Probably all views, values, customs, and morals should be respected as long as they don't hurt anyone. For example, in this country most people eat beef. In some religions, the cow is sacred. Believers do not eat beef. Can anyone say that is wrong? Many people believe that animals should be treated as humanely as we treat people. Some people feel that you shouldn't eat or wear anything made from an animal. Should someone else say they are wrong? Or would it be better if people would just say, "I don't believe in or agree with your views. But I respect your right to feel that way."

Chapter 8

Peer Pressure

Is peer pressure really low self-esteem and a lack of self-confidence?

Many people blame all the things that teenagers do on "peer pressure." Drugs, drinking, sex usually happen because of peer pressure. It is not because teens really want to do those things. People who study teens say that. Even most teenagers say that. Most people agree that teenagers are so eager for approval that they let other teens make decisions for them. They say it's because they want to be liked. Most teens are afraid that if they're not like everyone else nobody will like them.

Do most teenagers really believe that? It prevents them from making up their own minds and living by what they believe. Is it really peer pressure that pushes teens to do some of the things that they do?

Could it be low self-esteem and a lack of self-confidence? People who don't feel good about themselves don't trust themselves to make decisions. They're afraid that what they decide will be wrong, even though in their hearts they know they're right.

We blame peer pressure, but we should blame low self-esteem. We need to find out why teenagers have so little self-confidence. Then we need to find out: 1) how we can prevent that; and 2) how we can help young people trust their own judgment. What are you willing to do to develop your self-confidence? Try writing a short paper on ways to build self-confidence. Or make a list of the things that you can do to become stronger emotionally.

I Am, I Can, I Will

Here is an exercise to help you to see yourself. It can then help you see what you can do. Finally, it will help you decide what you would like to do with your life. There are three sections to fill in. They should be titled: 1) **I am**; 2) **I can**; 3) **I will**.

Under "I am" list all the things that you believe you are: For example:

I am

friendly	fun	athletic	sociable
smart	loyal	attractive	cautious
warm	sincere	brave	sensible
interesting	thoughtful	realistic	serious

Peer pressure doesn't have to make you accept the values of others, such as drinking or smoking.

Under "I can" list all the things that you do well or enjoy doing. For example:

I can

sing	play volleyball	make friends easily
dance	fix things	get along with others
swim	write stories	play tennis

Under "I will" list all the things that you want to do or feel that it is important for you to do.

I will

- work hard in school so that I can go to college
- stay in school
- respect my own body
- take care of my health and not take drugs
- not drink until I am of age and then only in moderation
- treat others with respect as I would like to be treated

Daydreaming

Here's another exercise to try that might help you become more sure of yourself. Let's call it **"What my life will be like in 5, 10 or 20 years."** Try to imagine your life a few years after high school. Will you have gone to college? Learned a trade? Gotten a job? Will you be married? Have children? See if thinking about how your life will turn out helps you to feel more sure about what you can do.

Chapter 9

Criticism

"Keep away from people who try to belittle your ambitions.

Small people always do that, but the really great make

you feel that you too can become great."

-Mark Twain

During your life you will probably be criticized. For some people, it's just their nature to be critical. Your self-confidence will determine how you handle criticism. Some people are critical because they were criticized when they were growing up. When people feel bad about themselves, they are often critical of others. It makes them feel better to bring others down to their level.

For example, people who feel bad about themselves may wake up thinking they don't look very well. They might say to the mirror, "Don't you know how to dress?" or "You shouldn't wear that"; or "Why did you get your hair cut like that? It looks terrible." Those kinds of people might then insult their friends because they feel so bad personally.

41

Do your friends pick on you and you wonder why? Perhaps they just failed a test or scratched up the family car. They probably don't mean to hurt you. It may just be the mood they're in. Sometimes when you're in a bad mood or worried about something, it is more difficult to be positive.

Parents are often guilty of giving too much criticism, too. They may complain about everything you do. They may say that they wish you were smarter. They may tell you that you're not as helpful as your brother or sister. It's hard not to feel bad. But just because someone says you are lazy or stupid doesn't mean that you are. It may just be that they had a bad day and are taking it out on you.

So how do you handle criticism? What do you do when someone criticizes you? Do you snap back at them? Maybe you ought to think about it for a moment. Then we'll look at some different ways to handle criticism.

What if someone said to you, "You have purple skin. You sure look funny." What would you do? Would you think that he or she was picking on you? Remember "self-talk"? When someone criticizes you, you should also use self-talk. If you were confident about yourself, you would automatically say to that person, "Don't be ridiculous. I know that I don't have purple skin. You must be drinking or smoking something funny." You would think that the person was kidding. Do you see that it's how you feel inside that makes you respond in a certain way?

What if you weren't feeling very good about yourself and someone said, "You sure are stupid"? You

"Whatever one believes to be true either is true or becomes true in one's mind."
-John C. Lilly

Criticism by parents can really come from their own childhood—or their mood at the moment.

might say, "How did he or she find out so quickly? I just met him/her." If your self-confidence were strong, you'd think to yourself, "Boy, he sure doesn't know what he's talking about. He's just being mean or nasty. I'm not going to pay any attention." You cannot change what people say or do, but you can change how you answer them so that the result is different. You have the power to change how they make you feel about yourself.

Chapter 10

Rejection

"There are no real successes without rejection. The more rejection you get, the better you are, the more you've learned, the closer you are to your outcome."

-Anthony Robbins

Some people feel rejected every time they are criticized. Being rejected can be very painful, especially if it comes from someone that you deeply care about. Regardless of how you are feeling at the moment, the message you get is that the person no longer cares for you. He/she doesn't want to be with you.

Rejection is a negative experience. Nobody likes the way it makes them feel. The first thought that goes through your mind is why. Did I do something wrong? Am I a bad person? Why doesn't this person like me anymore?

"Obstacles
are the
things we
see when
we lose
sight of our
goals."

-Lee Burgland

We feel rejection in many different ways. Sometimes when we are being criticized we feel that something is wrong with us. But as long as you like who you are, being criticized doesn't mean that you have to change in order to be a good person.

When your parents punish you, yell at you, or hit you, you say to yourself, "What's wrong with me? What did I do wrong? What did I do to deserve this treatment?" Sometimes when parents punish, you feel that they don't love you. It is really a particular behavior that your parents don't like. **Remember, it is not that they have stopped loving you.** Most of us lack the confidence to be able to say, "I know that my parents still love me. I know that I am still a good person. They're mad at me because I've done something wrong. But that doesn't make me a bad person."

Even the definition of rejection suggests something negative—"to discard." An author sends his book to a publisher, and it is rejected. He might send it to another publisher who loves it. In any kind of business, work may be rejected because it doesn't meet the needs of the company. Even on a farm, the fruit picked or the animals raised may be rejected because they aren't as good as the farmer wants. That doesn't mean that everything is wrong with the fruit or animal; it only means that they don't meet certain standards set by one person or one company. Many people have been fired and then gone to become president of another company. Many people in history have been rejected at some time in their lives and later gone on to do something great.

Rejection usually says more about the people doing the rejecting than about you.

Look at this list:*

• **Louisa May Alcott,** who wrote the book *Little Women*, was told to find work as a servant by her family.

• **Beethoven** handled the violin awkwardly. He preferred playing his own compositions instead of practicing his technique. His teacher told him he was hopeless as a composer.

• **Winston Churchill,** British Prime Minister, failed sixth grade.

• **Charles Darwin,** father of the Theory of Evolution, gave up a medical career begun at Edinburgh. He was told by his father, "You care for nothing but shooting, dogs, and rat-catching." Darwin wrote, "I was considered by all my masters and by my father as a very ordinary boy, rather below the common standard of intellect."

Babe Ruth struck out 1,330 times, but he also hit 714 home runs.

• **Walt Disney** was fired by a newspaper editor because he didn't have any ideas.

• **Thomas Edison's** teachers said he was too stupid to learn anything.

• **R.H. Macy** failed seven times before his New York store was a success.

• **John Creasey,** an English novelist, got 753 rejection slips before his 564 books were published.

If these people had let the rejection they received beat them, they would never have been successful.

---

*Sources: (Encyclopedia Britannica; Collier's Encyclopedia and Three Hundred Eminent Personalities by Mildred, Victor and Ted Goertzel.)

Don't Be Afraid To Fail

You've failed many times, although you may not remember.

You fell down the first time you tried to walk.

You almost drowned the first time you tried to swim, didn't you?

Did you hit the ball the first time you swung a bat?

Heavy hitters, the ones who hit the most home runs, also strike out a lot.

One way to handle rejection is to use self-talk. You have to say to yourself, "That person may believe what he or she says is true, but I know it's not. I may not be able to change what he/she thinks, but I know that I haven't done anything wrong. If that person doesn't choose to be my friend there is nothing that I can do. It hurts, but I know there is nothing wrong with me."

Make a list of some times when you have been rejected. Write down how you felt at the time. Did you feel hurt? Did you feel beaten? Did you feel like a complete failure? Have three headings on your list: 1) why you felt rejected; 2) how that made you feel; and 3) what self-talk you could have used to help you handle your feelings.

Forgiving and being forgiven can change your life for the better.

Chapter 11

Forgiveness

Even minor feelings of anger that have never been

resolved can keep you from having good relationships.

A person with self-confidence forgives the past. A person with self-confidence knows that if he/she remains angry, he/she will never be able to maintain self-confidence.

There may be many things that people do that hurt you emotionally and sometimes physically. Sometimes, it is hard to forgive those persons for doing harmful things to you. To be able to succeed in life, you have to be able to forgive.

Forgiving and forgetting are two different things. You may never forget the emotional or physical pain that you felt. But until you are able to forgive that person you will always be struggling with those feelings. You will probably never have a good relationship with that person. It is easy to say the words, "I forgive you," but it is not as easy to mean them.

One way to begin to forgive someone is to write that person a letter. You may not even mail the letter once it is written. Getting out some of your feelings and letting that person know even on paper how you felt can be extremely helpful.

So right now close the book and sit down in a quiet corner where no one will interrupt you. Think of all the people in your life that you are angry at because of something they've done. Make a list of those people. Include people who did something very serious to you or something minor. Even minor feelings of anger that have never been resolved can keep you from having good relationships. They can keep you from feeling good about yourself.

This is what should be in your letter: State the actual incident, when it happened, who was involved, how you were feeling at the time it happened. Tell how you're feeling now about the incident. For example: "Dear Melvin, I'm writing to tell you how deeply you hurt me when you said that you thought what I was doing was stupid. I respect your right to think differently than I do, but I did not appreciate your telling me that I was stupid for doing _____. I felt that you really did not care about me as a person. I felt that you didn't care about my feelings at all. I know we are still friends, but we have not been able to have the kind of friendship we used to. Until I'm able to tell you about it, our relationship will suffer. At this moment, I forgive you for what you said. I may not ever forget it, but I forgive you for hurting me."

After you have written your letter, think about how you feel about that person. Do you feel any closer to that person? Do you feel as if a burden has been lifted from your shoulders? Just think about your feelings. After you've read your letter over you might want to mail it. Sometimes writing a letter can be better than coming face to face with someone that you're angry with.

Many of us have trouble with our anger. We often don't know how to express those feelings. When we write a letter, we can say all the things that we feel without putting someone on the defensive. Another way of forgiving someone is to stand in front of a mirror and say the things that you might have written in the letter.

Look in the mirror and pretend that your image represents that person. Say, "John, I forgive you for hurting me. When you spread those rumors about me, it hurt me deeply. I felt that you really didn't like me or respect me. I've wanted to tell you how I felt for a long time. I forgive you." You probably feel a lot better now. You may be able to have a comfortable relationship with that person. Most of all, you will feel more confident about yourself.

Responsibility brings with it most of the good things of adulthood: independence, respect, and contentment.

Chapter 12

Responsibility

To succeed in life you have to learn to be responsible.

To develop self-confidence, you must first be trusted by others. To earn trust, you must show that you are mature enough to make wise decisions. But someone must trust you enough to give you the chance to make some decisions. It is hard to earn trust if you cannot show people that you can make decisions. If they won't let you, how do you earn their trust? This is a difficult part of being a teenager. People expect a lot from you. They want you to be responsible for yourself. But teachers and parents are often telling you what to do. They frequently make decisions for you. At the same time you're expected to learn to become a responsible young adult. That's a tough one, isn't it?

To succeed in life you have to learn to be responsible. You can't hold a job or get a raise or a promotion if you are not responsible. You can't keep a marriage together or manage a family without responsibility. Unfortunately, not many adults have learned to be responsible. That is why many things go wrong for so many people. Over the years you must show that you are responsible. Going to school, being on time, doing your homework and turning it in on time are all ways of being responsible. Being in by curfew time, helping around the house, and listening to your parents, also show responsible behavior.

A self-confident person cares about himself/herself and wants to earn respect from others. One way to do that is to be responsible.

Conclusion

You can be a winner. You already are.

We are born with self-confidence. We are born feeling okay about ourselves. Unfortunately, as we grow up many things happen that affect our self-image. When bad things happen, it can be hard to overcome the pain. Some people become shy or irresponsible. Others let criticism and rejection affect them and become depressed or angry. Their self-confidence is shaken. Sometimes it is difficult for them to feel good about themselves again.

We also receive a lot of positive responses from the people in our life. That makes us feel okay about who we are and what we can do. But for some reason, we seem to remember the unpleasant events in our lives more. That is why it is difficult to feel as if we can go out and "conquer the world." But it is not impossible to overcome those obstacles. It may take some hard work, but you can be a winner. You already are. You just have to start telling yourself that.

Time somebody told me
> That I am lovely, good and real
> That my beauty could make hearts stand still:

It's time somebody told me
> That my love is total and so complete
> That my mind is quick and full of wit
> That my loving is just too good to quit:

Time somebody told me
> How much they want, love, and need me
> How much my spirit helps set them free
> How my eyes shine full of the white light
> How good it feels just to hold me tight:

Time somebody told me
So I had a talk with myself, just me—nobody else
Cause it was time somebody told me.

> From *Hello to Me with Love: Poems of Self-Discovery*
> by C. Tillery Banks
> (Reprinted with permission of the author)

Glossary

attitude A way of acting, thinking, or feeling. John
had a negative *attitude*.

belief An opinion that someone has that holds certain things to be true. Leroy has a *belief* that
physical violence is wrong for any reason.

characteristics An appearance or way of being. Ron-
nie had the same *characteristics* as his father.

competition A contest or match in which someone or
a team tries to win. The *competition* between the
two boys was heated.

conviction A strong belief; the belief behind what
you feel or think. The politician spoke with *conviction*.

courage Bravery. Tawanda showed a lot of *courage*
when she was feeling really sick.

criticism Disapproval, finding fault. There was a lot
of *criticism* about the new rules.

defensive Feeling under attack. Diedra always got
defensive when her brother picked on her.

emotion A strong or specific feeling such as love,
hate, or fear. When Sara's dog died, she felt a
deep *emotion*.

emotional Showing emotions; easily moved to strong feelings. Connie gets so *emotional* when she watches sad movies.

honesty The state of being honest; truthfulness, sincerity. *Honesty* is the best policy.

inferiority A feeling of not being good enough or not as good as someone else. The kids who didn't speak English had a feeling of *inferiority* whenever they were around the kids who had already learned the language.

integrity Honesty, sincerity. Jose would never cheat because he has a lot of *integrity*.

irrational Not able to reason; senseless; unreasonable. When Roger gets very angry, he says *irrational* things.

perfection A person or thing that is perfect; of high quality. Jimmy was always dressed to *perfection*.

qualifications Skills or qualities held by a person. Eva had the right *qualifications* for the job.

qualities Personality traits. The teacher told Stanley that he had many fine *qualities*.

reject To turn away, turn down, or refuse. Ginny worried that the girls at her new school would *reject* her.

rejection The act of being turned away, turned down, or refused. Tyrone was so worried about *rejection* that he never tried to make any friends.

relationship A connection with another person. Example: friendships; steady dating; marriage; employer/employee. Antonio did not have a very good *relationship* with his boss.

responsibility The state of being accountable or answerable. Angela had a lot of *responsibility* on her new job.

résumé A list of one's employment and experience. Lynette's *résumé* was so good that they invited her in for the interview.

self-reliance Confidence in one's judgment. Steven's parents were proud of his *self-reliance.*

self-assurance Confidence in one's own ability. Some people thought that Vinnie was stuck-up because of his *self-assurance.*

self-conscious Embarrassed; ill at ease. Kevin was so *self-conscious* that he always thought everyone was laughing at him.

sincerity Honesty. Everyone thought that Reginald showed a lot of *sincerity* because he was always truthful about his feelings.

superiority Feeling better than another. John had a feeling of *superiority* whenever he was in the company of others.

traits Features or personality parts. Reba and her sister had similar personality *traits.*

values Beliefs; moral standards. Jennifer was glad that her mother had taught her good *values.*

For Further Reading

Carter, Sharon. *Coping Through Friendship*. The Rosen Publishing Group; New York, 1988. Carter provides information on developing support groups and networks that give mutual help.

Kramer, Patricia. *The Dynamics of Relationships: A Guide to Developing Self-Esteem and Social Skills in Teens and Young Adults, Book 1 and Book 2*. Equal Partners; Kensington, Maryland, 1990, 400 pages. These books, designed originally for schools, deal with such topics as Self-Esteem, Communication, Conflict, Dating, Love, Marriage, Sexuality and Parenting.

Kramer, Patricia. *The Dynamics of Relationships: A Guide to Developing Self-Esteem and Social Skills in Preteens and Young People*. Equal Partners; Kensington, Maryland, 1990, 144 pages. This book has three easy-reading chapters on Self-Esteem, Communication, and Anger and Conflict. It helps young people explore their own behavior, attitudes, and feelings about who they are and how to communicate.

McFarland, Rhoda. *Coping Through Self-Esteem*. The Rosen Publishing Group; New York, 1988. McFarland, who conducts workshops on the importance of self-esteem, provides strategies for developing it.

Powell, Barbara, Ph.D., *Overcoming Shyness: Practical Scripts for Everyday Encounters*, McGraw Hill Book Company; 1979.

Rayner, Claire. *The Shy Person's Book*, David McKay, Inc.; 1973.

Strenkle, Clare, *YOU*. Frank E. Richards, Phoenix, New York, 1966. This book was written to help teenagers better understand themselves and improve their self-control and social skills.

Zimbardo, Philip, Shyness: *What It Is, What To Do About It*; Addison Wesley Publishing Company; 1977.

Index

About the Author:

Patricia Kramer is president of Equal Partners, an educational consulting firm that conducts nationwide training programs, staff development, and workshops for schools, social service agencies, and national organizations. She has been a featured speaker at many national educational conferences, been a guest on national radio and television shows, and been featured in many educational magazines and other national publications. Ms. Kramer has received The Golden Apple Award from the Foundation for Self-Esteem "for making an outstanding contribution toward the development and furtherance of self-esteem" and was recognized by the District of Columbia Association of Counseling and Development for outstanding "Program Development."

Photo credits:

Cover photo: Barbara Kirk
Pages 2,8,20,22,29,39,43,47, and 54: Stephanie FitzGerald; pages 11,15,16,23,31, and 50: Stuart Rabinowitz; page 24: Barbara Kirk; page 32: Mary Lauzon.

Design and production by Blackbirch Graphics, Inc.